WILD WEATHER

by
Clare Oliver

Dangerous Drought

Forest fires result from summers of little or no rain. A spark from a train, a bolt of lightning or—more commonly—a discarded cigarette can cause wildfires that are sometimes impossible to control.

SUN SACRIFICES

Energy from the sun is the source of all life on this planet. Many early civilizations worshipped the sun. High on their pyramid-shaped temples, Aztec priests made grisly human sacrifices to their god of sun and rain, Tlaloc.

Tlaloc

POLE POWER

One of the most powerful spirits worshipped by Northwest Native Americans was the Thunderbird. Tribes often built tall totem poles in the bird's honor. Lightning was said to shoot from its beak and thunder to roll from its beating wings. But, most importantly, the Thunderbird brought refreshing rain to water the earth and make the plants grow.

SPRINGING A LEAK

The Chippewa Indians of North America told a story to explain springtime flooding. According to legend, the sun's heat was held in a bag during the winter. But each spring a mouse nibbled a hole in the bag. All the heat leaked out, melting the snow on the mountaintops and causing floods.

DIVINE INTERVENTION

Weather has such awesome power, it's no wonder some people in the past blamed, or thanked, their gods for it. To people in early cultures, extreme weather must sometimes have seemed like the end of the world.

Thunderbird totem pole

BUSY BEETLE

Ancient Egyptians thought a dung beetle, known as a scarab, pushed their sun god Re across the sky every day.

SONG & DANCE

In times of drought, special rituals are sometimes performed to bring on the rain. African rain magic includes dancing, chanting, sprinkling small amounts of precious water—and even spitting!

STRANGE FOREBODINGS

Some people rely on their own aches and pains to decide whether to carry an umbrella or not. Others base their forecasts on the behavior of plants or animals. Do natural signs give us clues to the weather? You decide.

BRAIN BONUS

When do grasshoppers get noisier?

a) when they are arguing
b) when snow is forecast
c) as the temperature rises

Which side of the leaf shows when a bad storm is approaching?

a) the topside
b) the underside
c) the inside

When do shepherds and sailors like to see a red sky?

a) at night
b) in the morning
c) on July 4

(answers on page 32)

FIR-LY ACCURATE

Pine cones are surprisingly sensitive to weather. When it is dry, their scales shrivel and open out. When rain is on the way, their scales absorb moisture from the air and close up. Flowers also react to the weather.

Open pine cone, dry weather

Dandelions snap shut if the temperature drops below 50°F, while the delicate scarlet pimpernel's petals close just before it rains.

MOO-VE IT!

It is often said that cows lie down when it is going to rain so that they will have somewhere dry to sit out the storm. In truth, they are just as likely to lie down when there are only clear skies on the horizon—and to remain standing in a rainstorm!

WAKE UP, WOODCHUCK!

Groundhog Day is celebrated in the United States on February 2 when revelers watch what the groundhog does as it wakes. Also known as woodchucks, some of these small furry creatures are celebrities. Pennsylvania's most famous, Punxsutawney Phil, is featured in Groundhog Day news accounts all over the U.S.

ME & MY SHADOW

According to folklore, if the groundhog sees its own shadow when it wakes up from its winter sleep, expect six more weeks of wintry weather.

BAD HAIR DAY

Many people swear their hair changes on humid days. Muggy weather makes curly hair curlier, straight hair hang flatter, and permed hair lose its bounce!

A cow expecting rain?

COTTONY CLOUDS

Clouds are one of the most beautiful features of the sky. Satell images from space show huge white wisps constantly swirling above the Earth. These massive collections of cold water or ice may look like fluffy cotton, but they're far from soft to the touch.

Earth from space

WET BLANKET

Every cloud is made up of billions of tiny water droplets or ice crystals. Warm air cools as it rises, which causes the moisture in it to condense into microscopic droplets of water. Clouds that form very high in the sky—where the air is so cold it's freezing—form snow clouds packed with ice crystals.

HEAD IN THE CLOUDS

Maybe no two clouds look alike to you, but scientists say clouds come in ten basic kinds and three shapes. In 1803, Luke Howard was the first person to sort the clouds into different types. He gave them Latin names that describe how they look.

CLOUD CALL

The highest, wispiest clouds are called cirrus, from the Latin for "lock of hair." Next come the cumulus clouds. These classic, intensely white mounds look like fluffy balls of cotton wool with a flattish base. They are found in the middle of the sky and their name means "heap." Finally, there are stratus ("spread out") clouds—flat, layered clouds that lie low in the sky.

Cumulonimbus

BRAIN BONUS

What do you call the cloud left by a plane in the sky?

a) an aeropuff
b) a contrail
c) a snakecloud

Which cloud appears as a series of small bumps, and what does its name mean?

a) mammatus (breast)
b) lumpus (hillock)
c) uncinus (hook)

What type of altocumulus cloud formation looks like fish scales?

a) sharkskin sky
b) whiting sky
c) mackerel sky

(answers on page 32)

RAIN AGAIN

The world's rainiest place is in Hawaii. Expect to need an umbrella on Mount Waialeale for all but two weeks of the year.

TODAY

TOMORROW

NEXT DAY

MIX & MATCH

Luke Howard also came up with words to describe what the clouds did. For example, the word *nimbus* was used for clouds that brought rain. The idea was to combine the Latin terms to create the perfect description for every cloud. So a cumulonimbus cloud is one in the middle of the sky that is large, fluffy, and brings rain.

Magnified ice crystals

FANTASTIC FLAKES

The next time a snowflake lands on your mitten, take a close look at it. Every snowflake is six-sided and made up of microscopic ice crystals, but that's where the similarities end. In fact, every snowflake is as unique as each of your fingerprints. No two snowflakes look the same.

BRAIN BONUS

What percentage of an iceberg is hidden below the ocean's surface?

a) 10 percent
b) 50 percent
c) 90 percent

How much of fresh snow is made up of air?

a) over 90 percent
b) 50 percent
c) There is no air; it is only made of water.

How far does a glacier move every day?

a) one to two inches
b) twenty feet
c) one mile

(answers on page 32)

HAIL & HEAVY

The biggest hailstones ever recorded hit Gopalganj in Bangladesh in April 1996. Each one weighed more than 2 pounds—ouch!

THE BIG FREEZE

Believe it or not, we live in a warm period in Earth's history. Climate experts say we are in the Holocene epoch. This period began about 10,000 years ago when humans still lived in caves. Before that was the Pleistocene epoch (the Ice Age), which lasted about two million years and included about seven "ice ages"—times when at least a third of the Earth was covered in moving sheets of ice.

WINTER WONDERLAND

Frost is pretty cool, but there's nothing like waking up to a thick blanket of freshly fallen snow. It's like finding yourself in a pristine new world never before touched by humans or animals. Now THAT's cool!

Snowman

CHILL OUT

Of course, the snowiest, coldest places on Earth are the North and South Poles. The ice there never really melts, except along the coastline. New snow just falls on top of the old, pressing it down into superthick sheets of ice. In parts of Antarctica the ice is over two million years old!

MONSTER MELTDOWN?

Even today there are tens of thousands of glaciers, mostly around Antarctica and Greenland. If all the frozen water locked up in these glaciers melted at once, the sea would rise by about 200 feet. Every major coastal city—including New York and Los Angeles—would disappear!

WHITE OUT

Severe winter weather can bring serious danger. Blanketing blizzards trap people in their own homes. Power cables collapse under the weight of the snowfall, leaving many without heat or electricity. In remote mountain areas, the sheer weight of snow can send terrifying avalanches tumbling down.

BRAIN BONUS

Where on Earth was the coldest-ever temperature (-128.6°F) recorded?

a) Amundsen, Antarctica
b) Bostok, Antarctica
c) Vostok, Antarctica

Which of these freezes when it's seriously cold?

a) your eyeballs
b) gasoline in a car
c) the sea

Approximately how many people die in avalanches in the Alps each year?

a) 15
b) 150
c.) 1,500

(answers on page 32)

AVALANCHE!

Avalanches occur after a sudden, heavy snow or in the spring when the winter snows begin to melt. A sudden movement or noise, such as a car engine backfiring, can dislodge the snow or ice and set it moving. The avalanche rapidly gathers speed and can thunder down the mountainside at over 200 mph.

WALL OF WHITE

Run quickly if you are ever faced with a shifting wall of ice and snow. Either the sheer weight of the impact or the freezing conditions alone are enough to make avalanches a very serious danger.

After an avalanche

MOUNTAIN MUTTS

Dogs have saved many lives in the mountains. Their noses can sniff out people—even when they are buried beneath several feet of snow. In a couple of hours, a pair of dogs can cover the same area as 80 human rescuers!

Rescue team

LICK OF LIFE

The most heroic dog of all time was a Saint Bernard called Barry. In the early 1800s, he saved more than 40 people in the Swiss Alps. He once rescued a boy who lay under an avalanche of snow. Barry gently licked the boy's face until he woke up, then carried him to safety.

THE NORTH FACE

Lightning strikes the Earth 100 times every second.

FAR OUT

Check out your chances of being stuck in an electrical storm. Light travels faster than sound, so count the seconds between a lightning flash and its thunderclap. Every five seconds equals about 1 mile between you and the storm. If you see lightning and hear thunder at the same time, you're in trouble!

Lightning over Arizona

Bela Lugosi as Frankenstein's monster

MONSTER FORCE

In the eighteenth century, some people believed electricity was the life force that made human bodies work. In Mary Shelley's famous horror story, Dr. Frankenstein sparks his freaky monster to life by harnessing electricity from a storm. We might take electricity for granted, but scientists who experimented with it in the early days would be astonished to see the amazing machines and gadgets it powers for us today.

THUNDERBOLTS & LIGHTNING...

Very, very frightening! What's more, there are about 40,000 thunderstorms on Earth every day!

CHARGING ABOUT

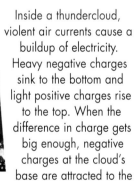

Inside a thundercloud, violent air currents cause a buildup of electricity. Heavy negative charges sink to the bottom and light positive charges rise to the top. When the difference in charge gets big enough, negative charges at the cloud's base are attracted to the positively charged ones on the ground or across the sky. Lightning flashes when the negative charges are released from the cloud.

ELECTRI-FRIED!

Roy Sullivan, a park ranger in Virginia, was struck by lightning seven times between 1942 and 1977. Over the years, he lost a toenail and suffered burns to his legs, stomach, chest, and left shoulder. His eyebrows burned off in 1969 and his hair went up in flames—twice!

13

BRAIN BONUS

What name is given to the still center of a hurricane?

a) eye
b) pie
c) sky

How fast must a wind be before it's called a hurricane?

a) more than 55 mph
b) more than 75 mph
c) more than 145 mph

What is a storm surge?

a) a swell of seawater just before a hurricane
b) an extra-powerful gust of wind
c) a doctor who treats hurricane victims

(answers on page 32)

The aftermath of Mitch

MONSTER MITCH

At the peak of its power, the winds of Hurricane Mitch raged at 190 mph. On the rampage in October 1998, it was the fourth-fiercest hurricane to strike the Caribbean in 100 years. Worst of all, two of the world's poorest countries, Nicaragua and Honduras, took the brunt of the storm. In the Honduran capital of Tegucigalpa, thousands died and tens of thousands lost their homes.

THE NAME GAME

An Australian weather expert called Clement Wragge had the idea of naming tropical storms in the nineteenth century. He chose boys' names from the Bible, such as Rakem and Talmon. Since 1978, hurricanes have alternately been given boys' and girls' names.

IN A SPIN

Hurricanes south of the equator spin clockwise. In the north, they whirl in the opposite direction—counterclockwise!

HURRICANE HORROR

The world's most terrifying storms are hurricanes.
Whirling winds race along at up to 225 mph,
carrying swirling thunderclouds and torrential rain.
Every second, a hurricane generates ten times more
energy than the atom bomb that was dropped on
Hiroshima, Japan, in World War II.

TROPICAL TROUBLE

Terrifying tropical storms sink ships, batter coastlines, and flatten houses.
They are known as hurricanes over the Atlantic, as cyclones over the
Indian Ocean, and as typhoons over the Pacific. Whatever you call
them, they bring big trouble!

BIRTH OF A KILLER

Hurricanes are born out at sea
where the air is warmer than the
surface of the ocean. Once storm
clouds have massed, they start to
spin. A hurricane can be over
600 miles across and contain
hundreds of thunderstorms!
These spiraling clouds are
monitored by space satellites,
but even with advance warnings,
hurricanes still do tremendous damage.

Hurricane Fran, 1996

WHIRLING WINDS

Terrifying tornadoes and suffocating sandstorms—winds can cause as much trouble inland as hurricanes do along the coast. Although most tornadoes tear along at just 30 mph, the winds inside them have been estimated at 500 mph! Tornadoes are fierce enough to break measuring equipment!

BRAIN BONUS

How many people died in the tornado that hit Bangladesh in April 1989?

a) 500
b) 900
c) 1,300

What is the nickname for the America midwest?

a) Windy Way
b) Tornado Alley
c) Twister Street

What are a pair of tornadoes called?

a) sisters
b) brothers
c) twins

(answers on page 32)

Tornado in Texas

SCHOOL'S OUT!

One of the luckiest escapes from tornado terror came in 1986 when 13 schoolchildren in China were safely set back down on the ground after being carried nearly 13 miles through the air. The children were unharmed, but their school was destroyed! Who said 13 was unlucky?

VIOLENT VORTEX

So, where do tornadoes come from? Like hurricanes, they start life in a thundercloud that has built up over a hot day. Then a stubby funnel of cloud begins to spiral downward. Once this twisting tube of air reaches the ground, it has become a full-blown and unstoppable tornado.

EGG-CITING DISCOVERY

Millions of years ago in central Asia, sandstorms in the Gobi Desert buried whole packs of dinosaurs alive. The hot sand kept huge unhatched dinosaur eggs perfectly preserved.

WHAT A CARRY-ON

When a tornado starts throwing its weight around, there's no telling what else it will throw! In the 1930s, a tornado in Minnesota actually tossed a train car about 25 feet through the air.

DESERT STORM

Wild winds and desert sands make a deadly combination, aptly named the dust devil. Sand blows around in the air with enough force to strip paint off a car! For centuries, the ancient Egyptian pyramids and sphinx at Giza were completely buried under tons of sand dumped there by sandstorms.

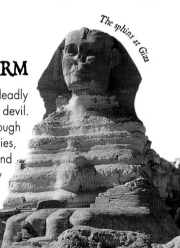

The sphinx at Giza

FREAK FLOODS

Flash floods even happen in deserts. In fact, more people drown in deserts in the United States than die of thirst.

Monsoon floods, India

BRAIN BONUS

What is the nickname of the Huang Ho River?

a) Stream of Sighs
b) Death River
c) China's Sorrow

Which place on Earth has the most rainfall each year?

a) Mawsynram, India
b) Bognor Regis, England
c) Mount Rainier, United States

How do trees prevent floods?

a) Their roots suck up rainwater.
b) Their roots bind the earth together.
c) The leaves act as an umbrella.

(answers on page 32)

RIVERS OF SADNESS

In 1998, heavy rains flooded China's longest river, the Yangtze, and nearly 3,000 people died. Experts say the flooding was especially bad because people had chopped down the trees that had supported the riverbank. When the Huang Ho overflowed in 1887, nearly a million people lost their lives. The 1887 Chinese flood was the worst ever recorded.

OH, NOAH!

Could Noah's legendary flood have been real? Experts say there really was an enormous flood about 7,000 years ago. It had a force 200 times that of Niagara Falls.

RAIN... AGAIN!

Believe it or not, floods kill more people each year than all the other natural disasters in the world put together. Most floods occur when rivers overrun their banks after filling up with water from torrential rains or melting snow.

TERRIBLE TOLL

In the tropics, people depend on the annual rains. In places such as India and Bangladesh, farmers need the precious water for their crops of rice and tea. But sometimes the monsoon (seasonal) winds bring too much rain. When the monsoon rains hit Thailand in 1983, 10,000 people lost their lives. As a result of drinking contaminated water, 100,000 people caught dangerous diseases.

Green frog

FLOOD OF FROGS?

It's not only rain that falls from the sky. Sometimes fierce winds, such as tornadoes, pick up animals, hurl them through the air, and drop them miles away. That might explain why there have been showers of fish, frogs, rats, and even pigs!

DEATH IN THE DESERT

A scary skull is often all that remains of an animal after a drought. Once all the grass has died and the water supply is dried up, many wild creatures become weak and die.

Steer's skull

FANNING THE FLAMES

As the plants wither and become tinder dry, the scene is set for wildfires. These are common in California, parts of Australia, and in southern France. Sometimes a lightning bolt sets off the fire, but more often it's human carelessness. Hot, dry winds fan the flames. A drought across the United States in 1988 caused a major fire in Yellowstone National Park.

Yellowstone fire, 1988

FLAMES & FAMINE

You may think torrential rain causes problems—
and it does—but things can also get pretty desperate
when the rain fails to fall.

HIGH & DRY

Most wicked weather is over quite quickly, but droughts go on and on. In places like the Sahel in Africa, there has been a long-term drought for over 30 years. And the Atacama Desert in Chile once went without any rain for 400 years!

WHAT'S COOKING?

The highest temperature ever recorded was in Libya, North Africa, in 1922. The temperature was 136°F in the shade— hot enough to fry an egg!

SMOKE & COUGHS

During 1997 and 1998, Southeast Asia suffered its deadliest drought in 50 years. Forest fires started easily, and the annual monsoon rains never came to put out the flames. For months, the fires raged out of control, choking the whole region with poisonous fumes.

PERFECT PRISM

One of the most glorious sights in the sky is the rainbow.
All sorts of myths surround this magnificent arch.

MYTH & MAGIC

Rainbow over France

For the ancient Greeks, a rainbow was the
path of the goddess Iris across the sky.
It was said to be God's promise to
Noah after the flood. And many
tribes—from the Masai of East
Africa to the Yuki of North
America—considered the
rainbow to be the robe of god.

COLOR THEORY

From the outside in, on a
single rainbow, the colors are
red, orange, yellow, green,
blue, indigo, and violet.
Remember them by taking the
first letters of this saying:
Richard of York gave
battle in vain.

SEEING DOUBLE

Sometimes, two (or three) rainbows appear in
the sky. The outer one is usually the least bright and mirrors the main
rainbow; it is red on the inside and violet on the outside edge.

OVER THE RAINBOW

Scene from The Wizard of Oz

Most of the classic film *The Wizard of Oz* was set somewhere beyond the rainbow. The weather played a starring role as it was a raging tornado that carried Dorothy and her dog, Toto, into the land of Oz. Of course, it's not really possible to go to the other side of a rainbow!

FLYING HIGH

If you're ever lucky enough to see a rainbow from the window of an airplane, you'll see something even more amazing than the Munchkins of Oz. Instead of appearing as a semicircular arch of color, the rainbow makes a full circle!

GLITTERING PRIZE

According to legend, at the foot of a rainbow you'll find a pot of gold. Easy money? Sadly, rainbows never seem to touch the ground!

BRAIN BONUS

What is a rainbow at night called?

a) a starbow
b) a moonbow
c) a nightbow

How long did the longest-lasting rainbow last?

a) about an hour
b) over six hours
c) five days

What type of "rainbow" is colorless?

a) a fogbow
b) a whitebow
c) a palebow

(answers on page 32)

23

HELLO, HALO

If you thought only angels wore haloes, think again! Sometimes, a thin, white ring like a halo appears around the sun or the moon. It happens when light bounces off ice crystals that are falling through the air. A similar effect is a corona. This is a fuzzy circle of rainbow-colored light seen encircling the sun or moon. But a corona is caused when light bounces off drops of rain, not crystals of ice.

Solar eclipse

TOTALLY AWESOME

Eclipses are one of the most amazing phenomena to experience. A solar eclipse happens when the moon's path places it in front of the sun, blocking its light from the Earth for several minutes. A chilly wind often blows as the temperature drops very sharply. The sky darkens and flowers shut their petals as if it is night. A solar eclipse can last up to about seven-and-a-half minutes.

SEEING TRIPLE

Mock suns, or sun dogs, are two bright points of light that appear at either side of the real sun. Sometimes, but only very rarely, the same effect happens at night and moon dogs are produced. Like haloes, sun and moon dogs are produced by light passing through ice crystals.

SPECIAL FX

Rainbows aren't the only stunning special effects in the sky. Tricks of light create some of the most wonderful sights on Earth.

QUANTUM PHYSICS

Auroras are extraordinary splashes of trembling color that light up the night sky around the North and South Poles. Aurora borealis, also known as the northern lights, appears in the far north and aurora australis (southern lights) in the south. Auroras happen when particles from the sun (called electrons) crash into particles of gas in the Earth's atmosphere. The result is a spectacular display of colored light

Aurora borealis

REAL-LIFE GIANTS

A special effect called the Brocken Spectre creates scary giants in the sky! This happens when the sun projects the shadows of people on a hilltop on to a nearby cloud.

PUMP POWER

Windmills have been used for hundreds of years to grind grain or pump water from below the ground. Today, there are about 250,000 of them around the world. Some still pump water, but there are also high-tech turbines used to convert wind power into electricity.

SOLAR SPEEDSTER

Energy from the sun (solar power) can be converted into electricity and used to run everything from pocket calculators to racing cars. The fastest car ever to have relied on sun power alone is called *Sunraycer*. In June 1988, it achieved a speed of nearly 49mph—a record that is still to be beaten.

GUSTS A-GO-GO

Windsurfer

Wind lends a helping hand when you're going places. The first sails on boats were probably made from animal skins, but by the time of the ancient Egyptians, people were using billowing sails of cloth. Today, some huge ocean liners have sails as well as engines. When the weather's windy, the captain cuts off the power and saves precious fuel. And of course, lots of people have fun using wind to power surfboards and yachts.

WONDERFUL WEATHER

Come wind, rain, or shine, weather can be put
to all sorts of good uses—including
simply making us happy.
Best of all, it's free!

Sunraycer

DREAM ON

Many solar-
powered vehicles
carry backup
energy. Honda's
Dream Solar
car uses solar power
for the first 55 miles, then switches over to a zinc battery that carries it
another 60 miles. The car holds the World Solar Challenge title, with an
average speed of 50 mph.

HOW SAD

It's scientifically proven—sunshine is
good for you and a lack of it is bad.
In winter, some people feel less happy
than usual. Scientists say that due to
insufficient light, these people may be
suffering from **Seasonal Affective
Disorder (SAD)**.

THE ESSENTIALS

At a weather station, there is usually a wind vane that determines the direction of the prevailing (strongest) wind. Air temperature is measured by a thermometer. Scientists also measure how humid the air is (how much moisture it contains) and how much rain has fallen. But, most important of all, meteorologists must watch the sky to see what type of clouds are forming.

Weather station

WEATHER WATCHERS

Forecasters gather all sorts of information to predict what the weather is going to do. They rely on weather stations dotted all over the planet. Weather balloons take readings from high in the atmosphere. In space, satellites send back more information. All this data is fed into number-crunching supercomputers with enough processing power to make sense of it all.

WEATHER WHIZ KIDS

OK, so weather forecasters often get it wrong, but what would we do without them? Meteorologists help ships and planes avoid dangerous weather and their forecasts allow people to get out of the way of deadly storms.

ANY WAY THE WIND BLOWS

Francis Beaufort knew the importance of observation. He was an admiral in the British Navy in the nineteenth century. He worked out a scale that would help sailors at sea guess the wind speed just by looking at its effects on the ocean. The scale goes from Force 1, when the air is still, to Force 12, when the wind speed indicates a full-blown hurricane.

THE PRESSURE'S ON

Early weather scientists spent a lot of time finding out about air. Before they did anything else, it had to be proved that air even existed. After all, no one could see it! By the 1600s, scientists had discovered that air pressure affected the weather. High pressure meant that dry, stable weather was likely, but a sharp drop in pressure meant wind, rain, and storms were on the way.

Weather vane

BRAIN BONUS

What was the name of the first weather satellite?

a) *Telstar*
b) *Tiros 1*
c) *Rosti 1*

When were the first automated weather balloons launched?

a) 1798
b) 1898
c) 1918

What does WWW stand for?

a) Wild Wombat Wrestling
b) Web of Weather Watchers
c) World Weather Watch

(answers on page 32)

SPIES IN THE SKY

Since the 1960s, satellites in space have been constantly taking photographs of the Earth. Weather satellites provide meteorologists with a view of the clouds they can't see any other way.

BUSY BALLOONS

Hundreds of huge, silvery weather balloons are released into the sky twice a day. Filled with helium, they rise slowly into the upper atmosphere. On board, robotic instruments take vital readings of humidity, air and temperature, and air pressure. The results are transmitted back to special radio dishes on the ground. This wasn't always the case. In the early days, brave scientists went ballooning up to dizzying heights to study the skies.

Meteorologist with weather balloon

SAT STILL?

Weather satellites come in two types. Some always stay above the same spot and are called geostationary satellites. Others circle the globe from pole to pole. These are called polar-orbiting satellites.

Meteosat *satellite in geostationary orbit above Africa*

SAVING LIVES

Satellite views of storms have made it possible to predict the likely path of a hurricane. Armed with such information, governments can forewarn people in dangerous hurricane zones and try to evacuate them. In 1992, millions of people in the Bahamas and the United States were evacuated before the arrival of the powerful Hurricane Andrew. Although fifty-four people died, without the warnings there could have been thousands more.

SIZING UP

When you see pictures of satellites in space, they seem to be really huge. In fact, most are no bigger than an adult!

BRAIN BONUS ANSWERS

p. 2 c) Indra. c) bullroarer. b) Huracan.

p. 4 c) as the temperature rises. b) the underside. a) at night.

p. 7 b) a contrail. a) mammatus (breast). c) mackerel sky.

p. 8 c) 90 percent. a) over 90 percent. a) one to two inches.

p. 10 c) Vostok, Antarctica, in 1960. a) b) c) Eyeballs, gasoline, and the sea will all freeze. b) 150.

p. 13 c) Lightning usually strikes tall objects. c) 500 times a year. a) Benjamin Franklin.

p. 14 a) eye. b) more than 75 mph. a) swell of seawater just before a hurricane.

p. 16 c) 1,300. b) Tornado Alley. a) sisters.

p. 18 c) China's Sorrow. a) Mawsynram, India. a) b) Their roots suck up rainwater and bind the earth together.

p. 20 c) Atacama Desert, Chile. b) banksia shrub. a) They contain flammable oil.

p. 23 b) a moonbow. b) over six hours. a) a fogbow.

p. 24 b) syzygy. c) seven. a) goddess of the dawn.

p. 26 b) 93 million miles. a) in Persia (now Iran). c) a photovoltaic cell.

p. 28 a) 1922. a) Evangelista Torricelli. a) quicksilver (mercury).

p. 30 b) *Tiros 1.* b) 1898. c) World Weather Watch.